SOUND *Artistry*
INTERMEDIATE METHOD
for SAXOPHONE

PETER BOONSHAFT & CHRIS BERNOTAS

T0025119

in collaboration with

DR. GABRIEL PIQUÉ

Thank you for making *Sound Artistry Intermediate Method for Saxophone* a part of your continued development as a musician. This book will help you progress toward becoming a more able and independent musician, focusing on both your technical and musical abilities. It offers material ranging from intermediate to advanced, making it valuable for musicians at various experience levels.

The many instrument-specific exercises in this book will help to support your personal improvement of techniques on your instrument, focusing on skills that may not always be addressed in an ensemble or in other repertoire. You will notice there are many performance and technique suggestions throughout the book. This wonderful advice has been provided by our renowned collaborative partners, as well as the many specialist teachers we worked with to create this book.

Sound Artistry Intermediate Method for Saxophone is organized into lessons that can be followed sequentially. As you progress through each lesson, it is a good idea

to go back to previous lessons to reinforce concepts and skills, or just to enjoy performing the music. Exercises include Long Tones, Flexibility, Major and Minor Scales (all forms), Scale Studies, Arpeggio Studies, Chromatic Studies, Etudes, and Duets, as well as exercises that are focused on skills that are particular to your instrument. You will notice that many studies are clearly marked with dynamics, articulations, style, and tempo for you to practice those aspects of performance. Other studies are intentionally left for you to determine those aspects of your musical interpretation and performance. This book progresses through various meters and every key. Once a key has been introduced, previous keys are interspersed throughout for reinforcement and variety. In the back of this book you will also find expanded-range scale pages and a detailed fingering chart.

We wish you all the best as you continue to develop your musicianship, technique, and artistry!

~ Peter Boonshaft and Chris Bernotas

Gabriel Piqué is Assistant Professor of Saxophone and Jazz Studies at The Baldwin Wallace University—Conservatory of Music. As a soloist and active performer, Piqué has presented concerts all over the world. He is the baritone saxophonist of the award-winning Fuego Quartet, which won the gold medal in the 2017 Fischoff National Chamber Music Competition and the 2017 Plowman Chamber Music Competition. Piqué also plays alto saxophone in the critically acclaimed touring saxophone sextet, The Moanin' Frogs, and regularly performs with The Cleveland Orchestra.

Alfred

alfred.com

Copyright © 2023 by Alfred Music
All rights reserved. Printed in USA.

ISBN-10: 1-4706-6655-3
ISBN-13: 978-1-4706-6655-2

Instrument photos provided courtesy of Jupiter Band Instruments/KHS America

Lesson 1

VENTING is opening a key to raise the pitch a note, **COVERING** is putting down a key to lower the pitch of a note. These actions often help to improve intonation. Often, the intonation of fourth-line D can be improved by adding the left-hand pinky key that is used when playing low B (not the right-hand pinky key). For the D♭ (C♯), you can vent using the side C key.

Fingering with covering: Fingering with venting:

1 LONG TONES

ALTERNATE FINGERINGS
There are multiple fingerings availble for these notes. Remember that side C to Bis B♭, and vice versa, is never a good choice. Always avoid sliding onto and off of Bis B♭.

2 SIDE C AND B♭

3 FLEXIBILITY—*Low and high notes should be played the exact same way. Find one embouchure and throat/tongue position where the entire range of the instrument plays with ease. Do not squeeze for the high notes or move the jaw for the low notes; they should all feel the same as the recommended mouthpiece concert pitches for each instrument (Alto = A, Tenor = G, Baritone = D).*

4 C MAJOR SCALE AND ARPEGGIO—*For all scale exercises that are written in octaves, practice each octave separately and then as a two-octave scale and arpeggio.*

5 C MAJOR SCALE STUDY

6 ARPEGGIO STUDY

7 ETUDE—*Play all etudes slowly with a steady tempo and good tone quality before speeding up. Always keep a good tone in mind and perform with musicality.*

Moderato ♩ = 100

mf

f

8 ETUDE

Deliberately ♩ = 108

mf

mp   *cresc.*   *rall.*   *f*   *a tempo*

molto rall.

9 ETUDE—*Practice this etude with two-bar phrases and then four-bar phrases.*

Legato ♩ = 80

mf   *f*   *mf*

p

10 DUET

Majestically ♩ = 82

mf

mf

Lesson 2

11 **LONG TONES**—*Often, venting can improve the intonation of third-line B♭ by opening the left-hand G♯ key. Third-line B and third-space C can be improved by opening the bottom right-hand side key.*

12 **A MINOR SCALE**

13 **A MINOR SCALE STUDY**

14 **ETUDE**

15 **ETUDE**

16 **ALTERNATE FINGERINGS**

| Ch. = Chromatic or Forked fingering | Bis = Bis B♭ |
| S = Side C | 1+1 = B♭ |

17 **CHROMATIC SCALE ETUDE**

18 **CHROMATIC SCALE ETUDE**

Moderately ♩ = 88

19 **ETUDE**—*After playing this etude as written, create or improvise a new ending for the last two measures.*

Lightly ♪ = 120

mf

Lesson 3

20 LONG TONES—*Remember to always have proper posture, embouchure, and hand position to promote performing with a beautiful tone.*

21 FLEXIBILITY

22 F MAJOR SCALE AND ARPEGGIO—*Sing or hum these notes before playing them. Internalizing the pitch will help develop your aural skills.*

23 F MAJOR SCALE STUDY

24 ETUDE

25 ARPEGGIO STUDY

26 ETUDE

27 DUET

Lesson 4

28 **D MINOR SCALE**

29 **D MINOR SCALE STUDY**

30 **ETUDE**

31 **ETUDE**

32 **DUET**—*Work toward matching each of the musical elements in this duet for a unified performance.*

Moderately ♩ = 100

33 **ETUDE**—*Play this etude with an eighth-note pulse until the rhythm is accurate. Then, transition to the dotted-quarter-note pulse.*

Legato ♩. = 60

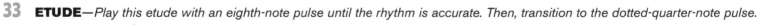

CHECKING FOR LEAKS
Play a first space F. Go back and forth pressing and releasing the G♯ key while playing the F. If you hear any change in sound or additional resistance while the G♯ key is being pressed, you have a leak. Fortunately, leaks are easily fixed because there is an adjustment screw, but it's best to take it to a professional just in case.

Lesson 5

34 **ETUDE**

35 **ETUDE**

36 **ETUDE**

37 **ETUDE**

Stately ♩ = 98

38 **DUET**

Maestoso ♩ = 72

39 **ETUDE**

Cantabile ♩ = 72

Lesson 6

40 **FLEXIBILITY**

41 **G MAJOR SCALE AND ARPEGGIO**

42 **G MAJOR SCALE STUDY**—*Using manuscript paper or notation software, compose a new scale study that you think is even more challenging.*

43 **RANGE EXTENSION**—*Often, covering can improve the intonation of higher notes starting with the second ledger line C♯. For that note and above, add the index finger of the right hand.*

44 **RANGE EXTENSION**

45 INTERVAL STUDY

46 ETUDE

47 ETUDE—*Practice this etude with two-bar phrases and then four-bar phrases. Experiment with the use of vibrato in this etude. Producing vibrato involves moving the jaw slightly down, then back up to create variations in pitch. When used appropriately, it adds warmth and can enhance your tone. Listen to recordings of great saxophone performers for models of vibrato. In addition, listening to and watching violinists (or other string players) is a great way to begin to understand the function and mechanics of vibrato.*

48 ETUDE

Lesson 7

49 **FLEXIBILITY**

50 **E MINOR SCALE**

Natural   Harmonic

Melodic   Arpeggio

51 **E MINOR SCALE STUDY**

52 **ETUDE**
Majestically ♩ = 88

53 **ETUDE**
Adagio ♩ = 66

54 ETUDE

55 ETUDE—*After successfully playing this etude, seek guidance from a teacher for ways you can refine your performance.*

56 ETUDE

Lesson 8

57 FLEXIBILITY

58 B♭ MAJOR SCALE AND ARPEGGIO

59 B♭ MAJOR SCALE STUDY

60 ETUDE—*If this exercise is not rhythmically even at the dotted-quarter-note pulse, try setting your metronome to the eighth-note pulse of ♪ = 180.*

61 ETUDE—*Be creative with the musicality of this etude by altering and adding your own dynamic markings.*

17

62 DUET

Waltz ♩ = 120

D.C. al Fine

63 G MINOR SCALE

Natural

Harmonic

Melodic

Arpeggio

64 G MINOR SCALE STUDY

Moderately ♩ = 100

65 ETUDE

Agitato ♩ = 96

Fine

D.C. al Fine

Lesson 9

GRACE NOTES are ornaments that are performed before the beat or on the beat, depending on the musical time period, style, context, and notation. The last example below shows how unslashed grace notes would be performed in the Classical period. Listen to music from various historical periods and notice the different approaches to the performance of grace notes.

Most often performed before the beat

Classical period, no slash. On the beat (in time).

66 GRACE NOTES—*Play these grace notes just before the main note.*

67 ETUDE

68 ETUDE—*An appoggiatura is a grace note without a slash that is played on the beat. In this exercise, measures 1 and 5, as well as measures 3 and 7, would be played the same.*

69 ETUDE

70 ETUDE

71 ETUDE

72 ETUDE—*Record your performance of this etude. Recognize the personal musical growth you have made from when you sight-read the piece. Think about the technical and musical ways your performance has improved. Do you hear a difference?*

73 ETUDE

Lesson 10

74 **LONG TONES**

75 **FLEXIBILITY**

76 **ETUDE**

77 **ETUDE**

78 CHROMATIC SCALE

79 CHROMATIC RANGE

80 MAJOR SCALE RANGE

81 DUET

Lesson 11

82 FLEXIBILITY

83 D MAJOR SCALE AND ARPEGGIO

84 D MAJOR SCALE STUDY

Moderately ♩ = 120

85 ETUDE

Adagio ♩ = 60

86 ETUDE

Allegro ♩ = 90

continued on next page

23

87 **ETUDE**

88 **ETUDE**—*After performing this etude, discuss the various elements of the musical work with a peer or teacher.*

89 **ETUDE**

Lesson 12

90 **FLEXIBILITY**

91 **B MINOR SCALE**

92 **B MINOR SCALE STUDY**

93 **B MINOR SCALE STUDY**

94 **DUET**

A **TRILL** is an ornament that is performed by alternating rapidly between the written note and the next diatonic note above. Sometimes you will see a natural, sharp, or flat sign with a trill, which means to alternate between the written note and the next altered note. Always check the key signature. Find various options of trill fingerings online.

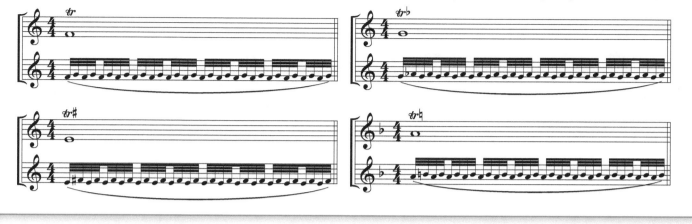

95 **TRILLS**—*Use your metronome to ensure an even and consistent rhythm.*

Evenly ♩ = 72

96 **TRILLS**—*Practice this exercise to ensure your trills are played evenly. Trills from 3rd space C or C♯ to 4th line D can be performed with the high E♭ palm key (soprano, alto, tenor) or the high D palm key (tenor, bari). Note: these fingering are very out of tune, so start the first few notes of the trill with the full fingerings and then switch to the trill fingering to get the "impression" of the correct pitches but the speed of the trill fingering. Once you are comfortable with this exercise as written, try playing it in cut time (𝅗𝅥=160).*

Presto ♩ = 160

97 **TRILLS**—*Practice measures 1–5 at a slow tempo to reinforce muscle memory, gradually increasing the tempo. This exercise will help ensure that your trills are played evenly.*

Presto ♩ = 160

98 **ETUDE**—*Depending on the style or historical context, a trill may start with an upper neighbor as shown here. Practice these trills with and without the upper neighbor. Also, grace notes are often used at the end of a trill. This ornament is also known as a nachschläge.*

Moderately ♩ = 90

Lesson 13

99 **FLEXIBILITY**

100 **E♭ MAJOR SCALE AND ARPEGGIO**

101 **E♭ MAJOR SCALE STUDY**

102 **ETUDE**

103 **ETUDE**

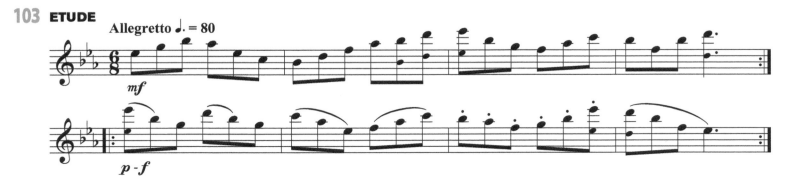

104 **DUET**

Andante ♩ = 102

Lesson 14

105 LONG TONES

106 FLEXIBILITY

107 C MINOR SCALE

108 C MINOR SCALE STUDY

109 ETUDE

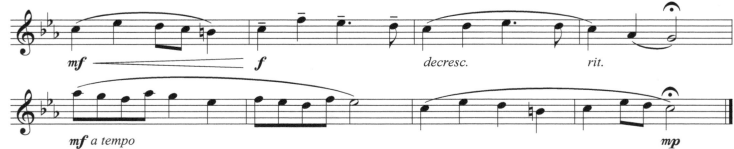

110 DUET

111 ETUDE

112 DUET—*While playing duets, both performers must listen critically to evaluate and adjust intonation.*

Lesson 15

113 **FLEXIBILITY**

114 **A MAJOR SCALE AND ARPEGGIO**

115 **A MAJOR SCALE STUDY**

116 **ETUDE**

117 **ETUDE**

118 LONG TONES—*Often, venting can improve the intonation of low E♭ and low D by adding the left-hand pinky C♯ key.*

119 F♯ MINOR SCALE

120 F♯ MINOR SCALE STUDY

121 ETUDE

Lesson 16

122 **DUET**—*When playing ♪♩, remember to think of a sixteenth-note subdivision.*

123 **ETUDE**

124 **DUET**—*What musical elements in this duet make it engaging? How does the form contribute to the musical work?*

125 **ETUDE**

Lesson 17

126 FLEXIBILITY

127 A♭ MAJOR SCALE AND ARPEGGIO

> A **TURN** or **GRUPPETTO** is an ornament that involves playing the written note, followed by the note above it, returning to the original note, then playing the note below it, and finally ending on the original note.

128 A♭ MAJOR SCALE STUDY

Adagio ♩ = 72

mf

129 A♭ MAJOR SCALE STUDY

Moderato ♩ = 112

mf

130 ETUDE

Andante ♩ = 80

mf

continued on next page

131 F MINOR SCALE

132 F MINOR SCALE STUDY

133 ETUDE

Lesson 18

134 LONG TONES—*After playing this exercise as written, try bending the pitch of the note under each fermata down a half step and then back to the written pitch. Try bending by only moving your jaw and embouchure. Then, try using only your tongue and throat. Note the difference in sound and choose the most appropriate way of bending for whatever style or genre you are playing.*

Slowly ♩ = 60

135 FLEXIBILITY

136 E MAJOR SCALE AND ARPEGGIO

137 E MAJOR SCALE STUDY

Moderately ♩ = 100

138 ETUDE

Andante ♩ = 108

139 ETUDE

Adagio ♩. = 60

37

140 **C♯ MINOR SCALES**

Natural

Harmonic

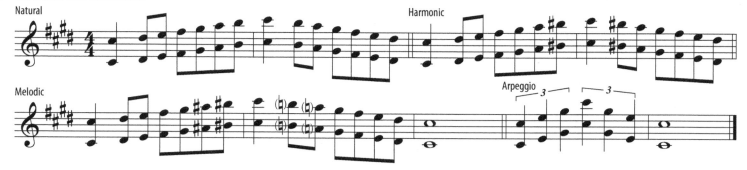

Melodic

Arpeggio

141 **C♯ MINOR SCALE STUDY**

Moderato ♩ = 108

142 **ETUDE**

Allegro ♩ = 120

143 **DUET**

Adagio ♩ = 66

Lesson 19

144 FLEXIBILITY

145 ETUDE

146 ETUDE

147 ETUDE

148 DUET

149 ETUDE

150 DUET—*Use critical listening to improve the performance of all musical elements in this duet.*

Lesson 20

151 **ETUDE**

Moderato ♩ = 88

152 **DUET**

Moderato ♩ = 108

153 **ETUDE**

Adagio ♩. = 80

154 **ETUDE**

155 **DUET**

156 **ETUDE**

42

157 ETUDE

Fanfare ♩ = 120

158 ETUDE

Majestic ♩ = 100

159 DUET

Majestic ♩ = 108

Lesson 21

160 FLEXIBILITY

161 D♭ MAJOR SCALE AND ARPEGGIO

162 ETUDE

163 ETUDE

164 B♭ MINOR SCALES

165 ETUDE

Lesson 22

166 **LONG TONES**

167 **B MAJOR SCALE AND ARPEGGIO**

168 **ETUDE**

169 **ETUDE**

170 **A♭ MINOR SCALE** *(enharmonic spelling of G♯ minor)*

171 **ETUDE**

Major Scales

C MAJOR

F MAJOR

B♭ MAJOR

E♭ MAJOR

A♭ MAJOR

D♭ MAJOR

G♭ MAJOR

C♭ MAJOR

G MAJOR

D MAJOR

A MAJOR

E MAJOR

B MAJOR

F♯ MAJOR

C♯ MAJOR

Minor Scales

A MINOR

D MINOR

G MINOR

C MINOR

46

F MINOR

Bb MINOR

Eb MINOR

Ab MINOR

E MINOR

B MINOR

F# MINOR

C# MINOR

G# MINOR

D# MINOR

A# MINOR

Saxophone Fingering Chart

= open
= pressed down

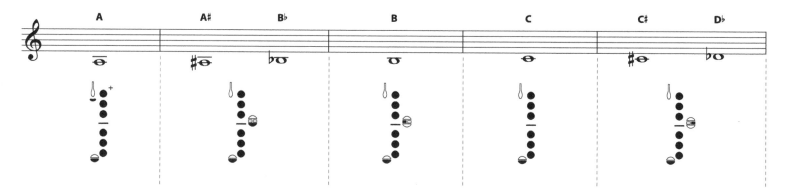

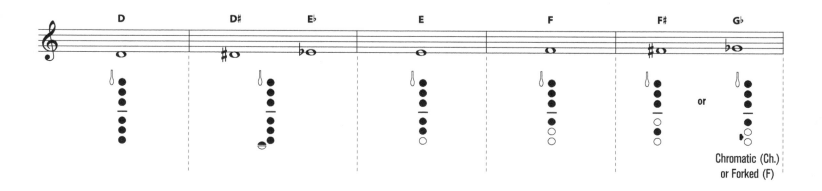

Chromatic (Ch.)
or Forked (F)

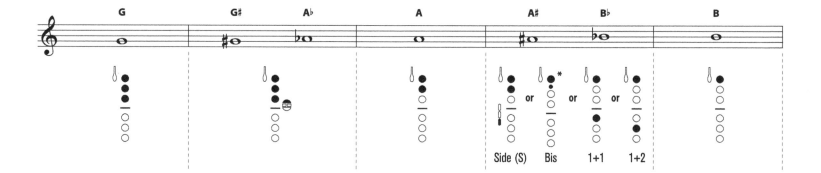

Side (S)　Bis　1+1　1+2

†This note is only available on some baritone saxophone models.

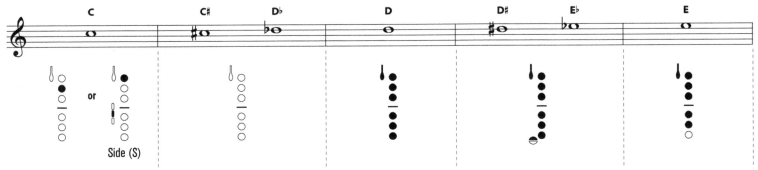

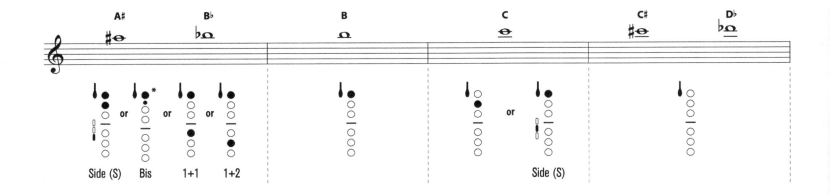

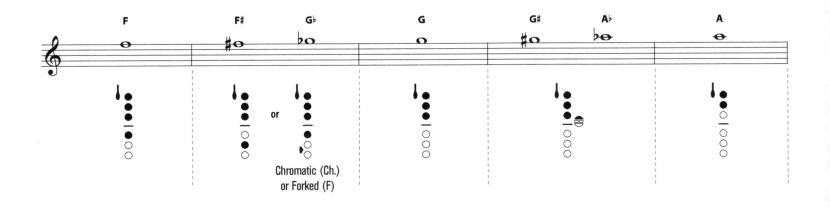

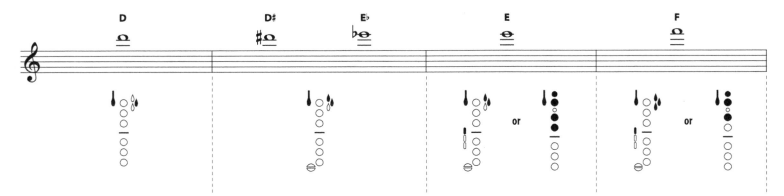

*The bis key is used for this fingering. This fingering should not be used in a chromatic scale.